ALTO SAX

15 TOP JAZZ DUETS

15 ALL-TIME CLASSICS ARRANGED FOR TWO PLAYERS
FLUTE, CLARINET, ALTO SAX, TRUMPET, TROMBONE

ISBN-0-7935-4922-1

HAL•LEONARD
CORPORATION
7777 W. BLUEMOUND RD. P.O. BOX 13819 MILWAUKEE, WI 53213

BODY AND SOUL

ALTO SAXOPHONE

Words by EDWARD HEYMAN,
ROBERT SOUR and FRANK EYTON
Music by JOHN GREEN

Bb Eb7 Dm7 Gm7 Em7 A7(b9) Cm7 F7 F#dim7
To Coda
To Coda
Gm7 Cm7 F7 Bb Dm7 G7(#5) Cm7 G7(b9) Cm7 F7
27
Bb Eb7 Dm7 G7(#5) Cm7 Cm7/Bb Am7 D7
Gm7 Cm7 F7 Bb Dm7 G7(#5) Cm7 G7(b9) Cm7 F7
35
Bb Eb7 Dm7 G7(#5) Cm7 Cm7/Bb Am7 D7
Gm7 Cm7 F7 Bb C#m7 F#7
D.S. al Coda
D.S. al Coda
CODA
Gm7 Cm7 F7 Bb
rit.
rit.

BYE BYE BLUES

ALTO SAXOPHONE

Words and Music by FRED HAMM, DAVE BENNETT, BERT LOWN and CHAUNCEY GRAY

F7
Amaj7
33
A
Cm7
F7
A
C#m7
40
F#7
B9
E7
A/C#
Cdim7
Bm7
E7
49
A
Cm7
3
F7
A
C#m7
3
F#7
57
B7
3
E7
A
F7
A

CALL ME IRRESPONSIBLE

from the Paramount Picture PAPA'S DELICATE CONDITION

ALTO SAXOPHONE

Words by SAMMY CAHN
Music by JAMES VAN HEUSEN

D7(♭9)
Gm7
Gm7/C
C7
F
31
F
F♯dim7
Gm7
G♯dim7
F
A7
D7
Am9
D7
39
Gm7
C7
Am7
D7
Gm7
C7
A7
D7
Gm7
Gm7/C
C7
F

CHEEK TO CHEEK

from the RKO Radio Motion Picture TOP HAT

ALTO SAXOPHONE

Words and Music by
IRVING BERLIN

2
A
Am7
28
3
F9
Cm7
F9
2
Bm7
E7
Fdim7
F♯m7
B7
Bm7
E7
36
A6
F♯7
Bm7
E7
A6
F♯7
Bm7
E7
A
Bm7
Cdim7
A/C♯
G9(♯11)
F♯7
B7
44
E7
Bm7
E7
D7
G7
F♯7
Bm7
Bm7/E
A

CHICAGO (THAT TODDLIN' TOWN)

ALTO SAXOPHONE

Words and Music by
FRED FISHER

D/A
Fdim7
A7
B♭7
A7
D
Em7
A7
28
D
G7
F♯m7
B7
Em7
A7
Em7
A7
Em7
C♯m7
F♯7
Bm7
B7
36
G
C9
D/A
A7(♯5)
D/A
Fdim7
A7
B♭7
A7
F♯m7
B7(♭9)
Em7
Em7/A
A7
D

I'VE GOT THE WORLD ON A STRING

ALTO SAXOPHONE

Lyric by TED KOEHLER
Music by HAROLD ARLEN

Dmaj9
F♯m7
B7(♭9)
Em7
A7
D
27
C♯m7
F♯7
F♯m7
B7
E7
Bm7
E7
Em7
A7
35
D
C7
B7
Em7
A7
D
F♯m7
B7(♭9)
Em7
A9
Em7
A7
D

IN THE WEE SMALL HOURS OF THE MORNING

ALTO SAXOPHONE

Words by BOB HILLIARD
Music by DAVID MANN

C6
Am7/G
17
C
Dm7/G
C
Dm7/G
C
Am7
Dm7
G7
Dm7/G
G7
Em7(♭5)
A7(♭9)
F♯m7
B7
Em7
E♭7
Dm7
Dm7/G
25
C
C7
C6
C(♯5)
C
Gm6
F
Dm7
D♯dim7
C/E
A7
Dm7
G7(♭9)
C6

LOVER

from the Paramount Picture LOVE ME TONIGHT

ALTO SAXOPHONE

Words by LORENZ HART
Music by RICHARD RODGERS

A♯7(♯5)
D♯m7
G♯7
E
C♯7(♭9)
F♯m7
B7
C♯m7
C7
Bm11
E7
41
A
D♯m7
G♯7
Dm7
G7
C♯m7
F♯7
Cm7
F7
Bm11
E7
A

MOONGLOW

ALTO SAXOPHONE

Words and Music by WILL HUDSON, EDDIE DeLANGE and IRVING MILLS

F7 Gmaj7 A13 Am7 D7
G7 Gdim7 G
33
Cmaj7 F7 Gmaj7
A9 Am7 D7 G Gdim7 Cm6/G G
41
G9
F#7 F7 E7 A9
D7 D#7 D7
49
Cmaj7 F7 Gmaj7 A9
Am7 D7 G7 Gdim7 Cm6/G G G7 Gdim7 Cm6/G G

SMILE

Theme from MODERN TIMES

ALTO SAXOPHONE

Words by JOHN TURNER and GEOFFREY PARSONS
Music by CHARLIE CHAPLIN

E♭7
F
D7
G7
Gm7
C7
33
F
F
G♯dim7
Gm7
D7(♭9)
Gm7
E♭9
F
D7
G7
Gm7
C7
F

SOMEDAY MY PRINCE WILL COME

from Walt Disney's SNOW WHITE AND THE SEVEN DWARFS

ALTO SAXOPHONE

Words by LARRY MOREY
Music by FRANK CHURCHILL

A7 F♯m7 B7 Em7 A7
D B7(♭9) Em7 A7 Dmaj7 G♯7(♭5)
33
A/G F7 Em7 B7(♯5) Em7 A7
Dmaj7 Am7 D7 G(♯5) G♯m7 C♯7 F♯m7 B7 Em7 A7
F♯m7 B7 Em7 A7 F♯m7 B7 Em7 A7 D

SOPHISTICATED LADY

ALTO SAXOPHONE

Words and Music by DUKE ELLINGTON,
IRVING MILLS and MITCHELL PARISH

F
F7
E7
E♭7
D7
G7
C7
To Coda
To Coda
Fmaj7
Am7(♭5)
D7(♭9)
Gm7
27
E♭7
D7
C♯7
C7
F
F7
E7
E♭7
D7
G7
C7
F
Am7(♭5)
D7(♭9)
Gm7
35
A7
B♭7
B7
C7
F
B7(♭9)
Cmaj7
C♯7
D7
G7
C7
Fmaj7
F♯m7(♭5)
B7(♭9)
D.S. al Coda
D.S. al Coda
Fmaj7
CODA

TANGERINE

from the Paramount Picture THE FLEET'S IN

ALTO SAXOPHONE

Words by JOHNNY MERCER
Music by VICTOR SCHERTZINGER

G#dim7 Gm7 C7 Gm7 C7 Eb9 D7
29
Gm7 Em7(b5) A7(b9) Dm9 Bm7 Bb7 F#m7 Gm7
To Coda
To Coda
C7 F D7(b9)
37
Gm9 C7
F Bb9 Am7 G#dim7 Gm7 C7 Gm7 C7
A7 D7
D.S. al Coda
D.S. al Coda
CODA
C7 G#m7 Am7
D7 F#m7 Gm7 C7 F F7(#9)

WALTZ FOR DEBBY

ALTO SAXOPHONE

Lyric by GENE LEES
Music by BILL EVANS

B7
Em7
C♯m7
F♯7(♭9)
Bm7
D7sus
Gmaj7
C♯m7
F♯7(♭9)
Bm7
E7
Fmaj7
B♭maj7
Em7
A7
D.C. al Coda
D.C. al Coda
CODA
Em7(♭5)
A7
G7
F♯m7
B7
G♯m7
C♯7
F♯m7
D7
Gmaj7
F♯7(♯9 ♯5)
Bm
Bm7
E7
G♯dim7
D/A
Ddim7/A
Em7/A
A7
D

WHAT'LL I DO?

from MUSIC BOX REVUE OF 1924

ALTO SAXOPHONE

Words and Music by
IRVING BERLIN

Dm7 G(♭9)
To Coda
C
G7sus
27
C
B♭7
C
To Coda
Dm7(♭5)
Em7 A7(♭9)
Dm7 G7
C
G
35
C
B♭7
C
Dm7(♭5)
Em7 A7(♭9)
Dm7 G7
C
Gm7 C7sus
43
F
Dm7
F
B♭7
Em7
A7(♭9)
D7
G7
D.S. al Coda
D.S. al Coda
C
CODA